3/09

Howl, Growl, Mooo, Whooo

A Book of Animal Sounds

Molly Carroll
Jeanne Sturm

Rourke
Publishing LLC
Vero Beach, Florida 32964

CAR

www.rourkepublishing.com

PHOTO CREDITS: © Cliff Parnell: Cover; © Larysa Dodz: Title Page; © Tessa van Riemsdijk: page 3; © John Pitcher: page 4, 6; © Lynn Stone: page 5, 9, 15, 24; © Davina Graham: page 7, 24; © AtWaG: page8; © Jerry Mayo: page 10; © Steve McSweeny: page 11, 23; © Tomasz Pietryszek: page 12; © Heinrich Volschenk: page 13, 23; © Nicholas Homrich: page 14; © Eric Isselée: page 16, 18; © Arkadiusz Stachowski: page 17, 24; © Alexander Hafeman: page 19, 23; © David Hernandez: page 20; © Nicole S. Young: page 21

Editor: Meg Greve and Kelli Hicks

Cover design by: Renee Brady

Interior design by: Tara Raymo

Library of Congress Cataloging-in-Publication Data

Carroll, Molly.
  Howl, growl, mooo, whooo, a book of animal sounds / Molly Carroll, Jeanne Sturm.
       p. cm. -- (My first discovery library)
   ISBN 978-1-60472-531-5
  1. Animal sounds--Juvenile literature. I. Sturm, Jeanne. II. Title.
   QL765.C357 2009b
   591.59'4--dc22

                                        2008025169

Printed in the USA

CG/CG

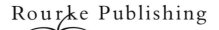

Rourke Publishing

www.rourkepublishing.com – rourke@rourkepublishing.com
Post Office Box 3328, Vero Beach, FL 32964

3/09 Pur.

Animals make many sounds.

The wolf howls,

HOOOOOWW

4

wL

And the panther growls.

GRRRRO

OWWL

7

The cow says, "Moooo,"

Mooooo

OOOO

And the owl says, "Whoo-Whoo."

Whoooo

Whooo

11

The bee says,
"Buzz Buzz,"

BUZZZZZ

BUZZZZ

Ruff

The sheep says, "Baa Baa,"

baaaa

Baaaaa

And the goat says, "Maa."

Maaa

18

aaaaaaa

Now tell us, what noises come from you?

Glossary

bee (BEE): A bee is a flying insect with a hairy body and four wings. Bees collect pollen to make honey. Bees use their long tongues to get nectar from flowers.

goat (GOHT): A goat is an animal with hooves, horns, and a beard. Goats are raised for their milk, wool, and meat. We can drink the milk from a goat, or we can use it to make butter and cheese.

owl (OUL): An owl is a bird with large eyes, a hooked beak, and sharp claws. Owls hunt at night. They eat mice and other small animals.

panther (PAN-thur): A panther is a large leopard with a black coat. Panthers are also called cougars or mountain lions.

sheep (SHEEP): A sheep is an animal with hooves, horns, and curly hair. Sheep are raised on farms. Sheep give us wool and meat.

wolf (wulf): A wolf is a wild animal that is related to dogs, coyotes, and foxes. A wolf will hunt for food in a pack with other wolves.

Index

Further Reading

Elliott, David. *On the Farm*. Candlewick Press, 2008.

Van Leeuwen, Jean, and Ann Schweninger. *Amanda Pig and the Really Hot Day*. Puffin, 2007.

Meister, Cari and Amy Young. *My Pony Jack at the Horse Show*. Viking, 2006.

Websites

www.seaworld.org/animal-info/sound-library/index.htm
www.alphabet-soup.net/farm/farm.html
www.naturepark.com/sound1.htm

About the Authors

Molly Carroll's family has an orange cat, and he frequently says, "Meow."

Jeanne Sturm and her family live in Florida, along with a very active dog, two friendly rabbits, and many colorful fish.